GREEN Is a CHILE PEPPER

A Book of Colors

By Roseanne Greenfield Thong
Illustrated by John Parra

Red is a *ristra*.
Red is a spice.
Red is our *salsa*
on top of rice.

red • rojo

Red is a ribbon.
Red is a bow
and skirts for
baile folklórico.

Orange are the marigolds on Day of the Dead.
Orange are the *platos* for special bread.

Yellow is *masa* we use to make *tortillas, tamales,* and sweet corn cake!

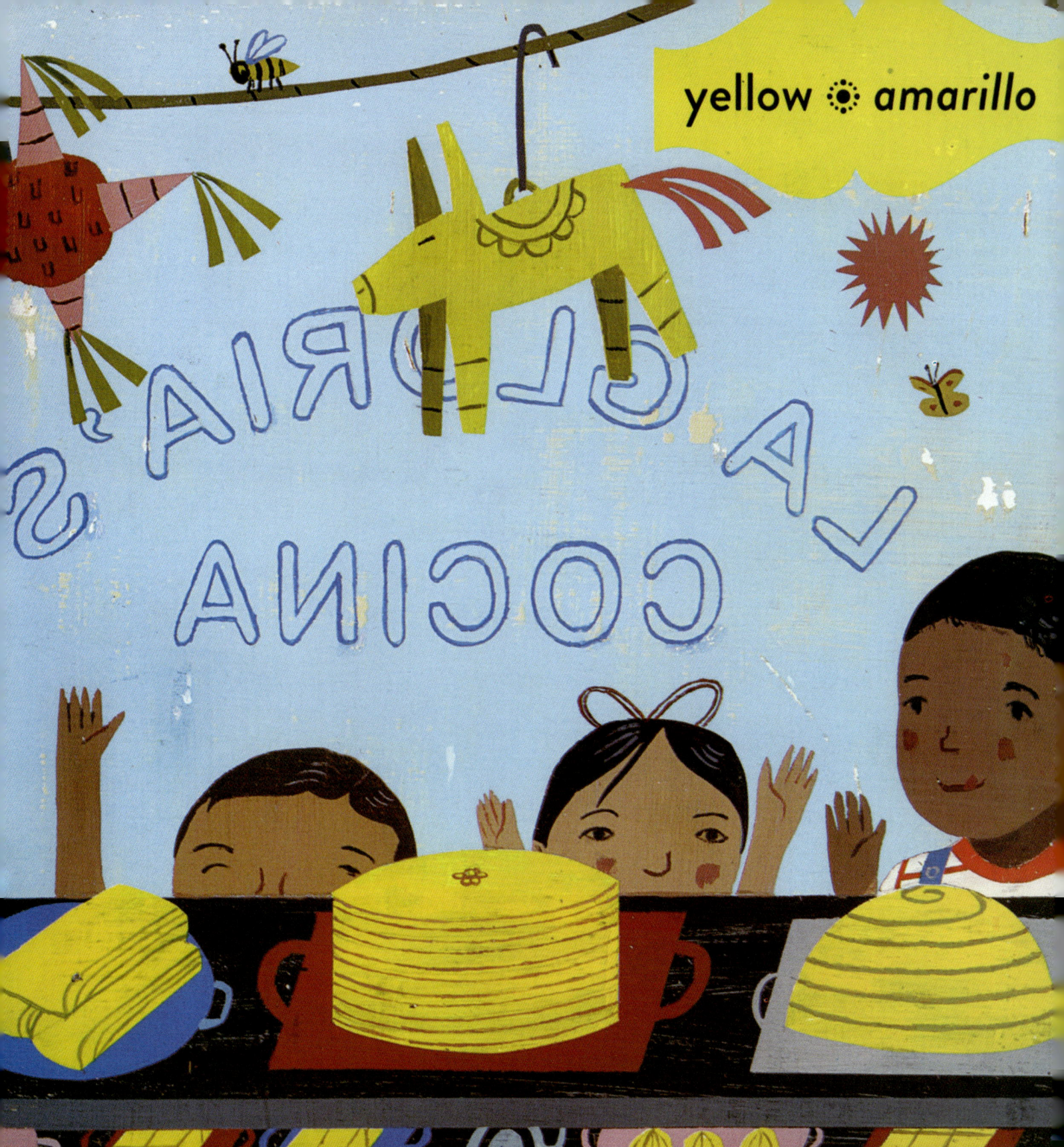

Yellow are the stars
that lighten the night.
Yellow are *faroles*
flickering bright.

yellow ⚬ amarillo

Green are the cornstalks.
Green are the pails.
Green is a bench
for *abuela*'s tales.

green ◈ verde

Blue is the endless sky above
and handmade crafts for those I love.

blue ● azul

Pink are *adornos*
and candles that glow.
Pink are *piñatas*:
Watch out below!

pink ○ rosa

Brown is a *churro*,
warm and sweet,
and homemade *chocolate*
—a special treat.

brown ◆ marrón

White are the doves
that chatter and coo,
and the *palomitas*
for me and you.

white ❂ blanco

In *ponchos*, *serapes*, and xylophones, too, these beautiful colors are waiting for you!

GLOSSARY

ABUELA: Grandmother.

ADORNOS: Decorations.

BAILE FOLKLÓRICO: Mexican folk dancing, known for heel stomping and swirling skirts. Each part of Mexico has a different dance costume, which can include ribbons, bows, fancy hair pieces, and shawls for women; and colored ties, belts, wide-brimmed hats, and boots for men.

CALAVERAS: Sugar skulls given as gifts or tokens of love, and placed on family altars for the Day of the Dead. The skulls (made of hard, compacted granulated sugar) are decorated with colored sugar frosting and often have names on the foreheads.

CHILES: Chiles come in many colors, including green, red, orange, yellow, and purple. Two popular green chiles are *poblanos* and *jalapeños*.

CHOCOLATE: Mexico is the birthplace of chocolate, pronounced *choh-coh-LAH-tay* in Spanish. The ancient Aztecs enjoyed it as a hot drink mixed with vanilla and chile pepper. Later, Europeans sweetened it by adding sugar and milk and removing the pepper. Mexican chocolate comes in bars, discs, syrup, and powder, and is used in a special meat sauce called *mole*.

CHURROS: Long, thin doughnut-like snacks that are fried until crunchy and sprinkled with cinnamon sugar.

DÍA DE LOS MUERTOS (Day of the Dead): On the first and second of November every year, to remember and honor the dead, cemetery graves are decorated with bright marigold flowers, candles, and a sweet bread called *pan de muertos*.

FAROLES: Lanterns made of colorful paper with a lit candle inside. They are used for nine nights before Christmas during *posadas*, or processions through the village, when participants stop at different homes to sing carols and enjoy food.

FERIA: Held during holidays, *ferias* are carnivals that often include rodeos, rides, food stalls, and game booths for winning prizes.

MASA: A cornmeal dough used for foods like *tamales* and *tortillas*.

MARIMBA: A Mexican xylophone with wooden keys, played by several musicians at the same time by hitting the wooden keys with mallets. Nowadays, toy xylophones are made with rainbow-colored keys.

OJOS DE DIOS (God's Eyes): Ancient symbols made by weaving colored yarn around two crossed sticks. The center of the "eye" is made when a child is born. Each year, a bit of yarn is added until the child turns five, at which point the eye is complete.

PALOMITAS: Meaning "little doves," it is also the word for popcorn, probably because the puffed, white kernels sound like flapping wings when they fly out of a pot.

PAN DE MUERTOS: This sweet bread known as "bread of the dead" is baked specially for Day of the Dead. It is often shaped like a skull and covered with frosting to resemble skeleton bones.

PIÑATAS: Containers made from papier-mâché, covered with colorful paper, and filled with candy or toys. Breaking a hanging *piñata* is a favorite party game. Blindfolded children take turns hitting it with